CW00495654

THE RISEN CHRIST

Jesus' Final Words on Earth

8 STUDIES FOR INDIVIDUALS OR GROUPS

LifeGuide®
BIBLE STUDIES

BILL WEIMER

IVP Connect
An imprint of InterVarsity Press
Downers Grove, Illinois

InterVarsity Press
P.O. Box 1400, Downers Grove, IL 60515-1426
ivpress.com
email@ivpress.com

InterVarsity Press® is the book-publishing division of InterVarsity Christian Fellowship/USA®, a movement of students and faculty active on campus at hundreds of universities, colleges, and schools of nursing in the United States of America, and a member movement of the International Fellowship of Evangelical Students. For information about local and regional activities, visit intervarsity.org.

Cover design: Cindy Kiple
Interior design: Jeanna Wiggins
Cover image: empty tomb: © joshblake / iStock / Getty Images Plus

ISBN 978-0-8308-3116-6 (print)
ISBN 978-0-8308-6435-5 (digital)

Printed in the United States of America ♾

InterVarsity Press is committed to ecological stewardship and to the conservation of natural resources in all our operations. This book was printed using sustainably sourced paper.

P 17 16 15 14 13 12 11 10 9 8 7 6 5 4 3 2 1
Y 33 32 31 30 29 28 27 26 25 24 23 22 21 20 19

CONTENTS

GETTING THE MOST OUT OF *THE RISEN CHRIST*

If you were leaving loved ones, friends, or colleagues, what last words of encouragement or farewell would you give them?

Jesus, while dying on the cross, uttered several statements that are often called "The Last Words of Jesus." During the Christian church season of Lent (the forty days between Ash Wednesday and Easter Sunday), Christians meditate on these words, various worship services focus on them, and pastors speak on them.

- "Father, forgive them, for they do not know what they are doing." (Luke 23:34)
- "Today you will be with me in paradise." (Luke 23:43)
- "Woman, here is your son. . . . Here is your mother." (John 19:26-27)
- "My God, my God, why have you forsaken me?" (Matthew 27:46)
- "I am thirsty." (John 19:28)
- "It is finished." (John 19:30)
- "Father, into your hands I commit my spirit." (Luke 23:46)

But his words from the cross are *not* Jesus' last words on earth.

Jesus appeared to his fearful and questioning disciples, encouraged them, and gave them his final instructions *after* his resurrection from the dead. In various settings and at different times, Jesus interacted with many of his followers to show them he was alive. His postresurrection dialogues with these women and men truly are *Jesus' last words*!

You may have questions or doubts about faith. You may have discussed spiritual topics or talked with others about Jesus. You may sometimes feel religiously locked into past concepts or socially locked out from people—even embarrassed or fearful about how others perceive you and your spiritual beliefs or questions. You may wonder, *Can Jesus really affect my life?*

Through these Bible studies, you will meet the risen Jesus Christ and hear his words. May he encounter you in your life situations, encourage your faith and trust in him, and excite you about engaging others in discussions about Jesus.

SUGGESTIONS FOR INDIVIDUAL STUDY

1. As you begin each study, pray that God will speak to you through his Word.

2. Read the introduction to the study and respond to the personal reflection question or exercise. This is designed to help you focus on God and on the theme of the study.

3. Each study deals with a particular passage so that you can delve into the author's meaning in that context. Read and re-read the passage to be studied. The questions are written using the language of the New International Version, so you may wish to use that version of the Bible. The New Revised Standard Version is also recommended.

4. This is an inductive Bible study, designed to help you discover for yourself what Scripture is saying. The study includes three types of questions. Observation questions ask about the basic facts: who, what, when, where, and how. Interpretation questions delve into the meaning of the passage. Application questions help you discover the implications of the text for growing in Christ. These three keys unlock the treasures of Scripture.

Write your answers to the questions in the spaces provided or in a personal journal. Writing can bring clarity and deeper understanding of yourself and of God's Word.

5. It might be good to have a Bible dictionary handy. Use it to look up any unfamiliar words, names, or places.

6. Use the prayer suggestion to guide you in thanking God for what you have learned and to pray about the applications that have come to mind.

7. You may want to go on to the suggestion under "Now or Later," or you may want to use that idea for your next study.

SUGGESTIONS FOR MEMBERS OF A GROUP STUDY

1. Come to the study prepared. Follow the suggestions for individual study mentioned above. You will find that careful preparation will greatly enrich your time spent in group discussion.

2. Be willing to participate in the discussion. The leader of your group will not be lecturing. Instead, he or she will be encouraging the members of the group to discuss what they have learned. The leader will be asking the questions that are found in this guide.

3. Stick to the topic being discussed. Your answers should be based on the verses that are the focus of the discussion and not on outside authorities such as commentaries or speakers. These studies focus on a particular passage of Scripture. Only rarely should you refer to other portions of the Bible. This allows for everyone to participate in in-depth study on equal ground.

4. Be sensitive to the other members of the group. Listen attentively when they describe what they have learned. You may be surprised by their insights! Each question assumes a variety of answers. Many questions do not have "right" answers, particularly questions that aim at meaning or application. Instead the questions push us to explore the passage more thoroughly.

When possible, link what you say to the comments of others. Also, be affirming whenever you can. This will encourage some of the more hesitant members of the group to participate.

5. Be careful not to dominate the discussion. We are sometimes so eager to express our thoughts that we leave too little opportunity for others to respond. By all means participate! But allow others to also.

6. Expect God to teach you through the passage being discussed and through the other members of the group. Pray that you will have an enjoyable and profitable time together, but also that as a result of the study you will find ways that you can take action individually or as a group.

7. Remember that anything said in the group is considered confidential and should not be discussed outside the group unless specific permission is given to do so.

8. If you are the group leader, you will find additional suggestions at the back of the guide.

ONE

WHO ARE YOU LOOKING FOR?

John 20:1-18

In 2010, it was discovered that some sixty-five thousand burial sites in Arlington National Cemetery—almost one-fourth of the military veterans' gravesites—had been grossly mismanaged. There were hundreds of unmarked graves in these hallowed grounds. Headstones were labeled incorrectly. Graves were found to be empty. Burial remains were moved without family knowledge or permission. Most of these inexcusable mistakes were done years ago. However, several gravesites involved military personnel killed in the more recent Iraq and Afghanistan wars. How shocking—at our nation's most-revered cemetery!

One appalling example concerned the cremains urn of Air Force Master Sgt. Marion Gabe, who served as an operating-room nurse during the Vietnam War and again in Operation Desert Storm. This urn was buried on top of another veteran's body. When the family of this latter service member visited the site, they discovered Gabe's headstone—not their loved one's! So cemetery workers relocated Gabe's urn and headstone, reburying her at another site without notifying her family. Thus, when Gabe's loved ones traveled to visit her burial site, her cremains were gone.

Group Discussion. Why is such burial mismanagement at Arlington, or any cemetery, so upsetting to families, veterans, and all of us?

Personal Reflection. Have you ever sought the grave of a family member or close friend and had difficulty finding the precise burial location? What were your thoughts and feelings as you searched for the site and then finally found it?

In the first century, Jewish women would anoint a dead body with spices to assist the natural decaying process. The women in this passage loved and supported Jesus' life and ministry. They witnessed his agonizing death. Now they had come to anoint his body, in accordance with Jewish burial practices. They sought a dead Jesus, but a surprise awaited them! *Read John 20:1-18.*

1. Imagine you are one of Jesus' disciples during the time of his crucifixion. What would you think about his death and your future after it?

2. When Mary Magdalene arrived at the tomb, what does she expect to see, and what persons does she encounter in the predawn darkness?

3. How do Mary's reactions to the empty tomb compare to those of Peter and "the other disciple" (vv. 1-10)?

4. "Mary stood outside the tomb crying" (v. 11). Do you think this was an appropriate response after all she had learned about Jesus? Why or why not?

5. Mary is asked two questions at the empty tomb (vv. 11-15). How does she reply to both queries and why?

6. How is Mary affected when Jesus calls her by name (vv. 16-17)?

7. Scripture indicates that the Lord also knows you—your name, circumstances, concerns, joys, and struggles. How does this truth affect your response to Jesus?

8. What do you think Jesus meant when he said to Mary, "Do not hold on to me" (v. 17)?

9. How does Jesus indicate his intimate relationship with God and his disciples?

10. If you, like Mary, have had a surprise encounter with Jesus, describe how this happened.

How did this affect or change you?

11. What did Mary do after interacting with Jesus?

12. How have Jesus' words to Mary Magdalene encouraged you in your faith?

Express your thanks and praise to God for this climax to Jesus' life and work on earth, and tell God your reactions to Jesus' resurrection!

NOW OR LATER

At times everyone feels disappointed, discouraged, depressed, or even defeated. What have you learned about Jesus from his encounter with Mary Magdalene?

TWO

WHAT ARE YOU DISCUSSING?

Luke 24:13-49

In his autobiography, *The Prince of Darkness,* famous syndicated columnist Robert Novak tells of a dramatic spiritual experience he had at Syracuse University in 1996. At the dinner before he was to speak, he had an unexpected spiritual encounter with a young woman sitting across the table.

A religious agnostic for decades, Novak noticed she was wearing a gold cross. He asked if she was a Catholic. She answered yes, and asked if he was. He replied no, but that he and his wife had been going to church the past four years. The young lady then asked if he planned to join the church. He replied no, not at this time. Her reply startled him, "Mr. Novak, life is short but eternity is forever!"

Novak said he was shaken throughout dinner and his speech. After the event, he tried to find this young woman, but could not. This stranger, who he had never seen and would never see again, challenged his vague religious beliefs. Years later he reflected that the Holy Spirit was speaking to him, and this encounter climaxed his years of spiritual void—culminating in his 1998 conversion.

Group Discussion. Have you ever talked with someone, only to learn later that this person was well known or famous? When and where? How did you respond during your encounter and then afterward?

Personal Reflection. Has a stranger ever engaged you in spiritual conversation that startled you, or has God ever encountered you unexpectedly in life? How did either of these occur, and what resulted?

Many people know some facts and information about Jesus, but do not have a clear faith commitment to him. In this passage, the risen Jesus Christ engages two such individuals and enables them to know him personally—causing a U-turn in their lives. *Read Luke 24:13-32.*

1. It is the annual spring Jewish Passover festival weekend, when thousands made a religious pilgrimage to Jerusalem. In this text as two people are walking, Jesus comes alongside them. What might have been some reasons they did not recognized him?

2. As Jesus engages them, what does he ask and learn?

3. How do you start conversations with those interested in or unclear about religious beliefs?

4. Why do you think Jesus opens with questions instead of immediate theological statements or claims about himself?

5. As these three walk together, the spiritual discussion reveals the understanding—or lack thereof—these two have concerning Jesus. What do they know and understand about him?

6. What things about Jesus do you know and believe, and what things about him are you not sure about but would like to discuss or study more?

7. As they arrive at Emmaus, why do you think Jesus indicates he will continue his journey, and why did they urge him to stay with them?

8. What happens in the disciples' home, and why do they finally recognize him at their table (vv. 30-31)?

9. After Jesus interacted with these two in their home, why and in what ways did they make a U-turn?

10. *Read Luke 24:33-49.* What occurs after the two disciples reversed direction and reunited with disciples in Jerusalem?

11. How does Jesus communicate with them to confirm that he is the risen Messiah?

12. Jesus wants his disciples to see he is risen and alive. But what does he also want them—and us—to believe and bear witness to (see vv. 44-49)?

13. By studying this passage, how have you modified and grown in your knowledge and your relationship with Jesus?

Thank the Lord for Scriptures that anticipate (in the Old Testament prophecies) and explain (in the New Testament accounts, especially the Gospels) the coming of Jesus the Messiah. Thank God for the ways Jesus has encountered you and caused U-turns in your life.

NOW OR LATER

In what situations and settings have you encountered Jesus? For example:

- doing your daily activities and interpersonal relations
- talking and fellowshipping with Christians
- studying the Bible alone or in a group discussion
- praying alone or with others in a group
- attending and participating in a worship service
- receiving Communion
- hearing or singing inspirational music, hymns, or songs

THREE

I AM SENDING YOU

John 20:19-23

The US Department of State's *Diplomacy Dictionary* defines an ambassador as the "chief of a diplomatic mission; the ranking official diplomatic representative of the country to the country to which she/he is appointed, and the personal representative of her/his own head of state to the head of state of the host country."

Merriam-Webster Dictionary gives these definitive phrases and explanations of an ambassador: (1) "An official envoy; *especially*: a diplomatic agent . . . representative of his or her own government and sovereign or appointed for a special often temporary assignment," (2) "an authorized messenger."

As we will learn in this study, Jesus sent out ambassadors—his disciples—to represent him and communicate his good news. The Greek word *apostolos* ("apostle") in the New Testament refers originally to the twelve apostles, who Jesus called, taught, commissioned, and empowered to proclaim the gospel and to establish his church.

Group Discussion. To be an effective ambassador for a country, what must a person know and do?

Personal Reflection. Have you ever been sent by someone on a unique assignment? Describe your experience. What was its purpose? How were you to conduct yourself? How well were you received?

After his postresurrection appearances over forty days, Jesus will ascend from earth. But first he must solidify his disciples' faith in him as the risen Messiah and Lord, and instruct them about the mission he is assigning them. *Read John 20:19-23.*

1. Summarize why the disciples had locked the door and were frightened of the Jewish leaders on Easter Sunday morning.

2. How did Jesus appear among the disciples, and what does this tell you about his postresurrection condition?

3. Jesus greets them with "Peace be with you" (v. 19). Why do you think he repeats this again to them (v. 21)?

4. When Jesus encountered them in their locked room, they were "overjoyed" (v. 20), but what other emotions might they have felt or thought—and why?

5. In what manner (Jesus' person) and for what purposes (Jesus' work) did God send Jesus into the world?

6. Why is Jesus sending his followers into the world?

7. Who specifically can you be an ambassador to on behalf of Jesus Christ?

8. Soon, at Pentecost (Acts 2), the Holy Spirit will come upon many believers, as foretold by an Old Testament prophet (Joel 2:28-32). In our text, what do you think Jesus is implying when he says to his disciples, "Receive the Holy Spirit" (v. 22)?

9. Why is the Holy Spirit critical for anyone who is being "sent" on a mission or ministry by the Lord?

10. What do you think Jesus means by his statement about "forgiving sins" in verse 23?

11. Who forgives our sins, through whom, and by what action of Jesus (also see Mark 2:5, 10)?

12. Some people have difficulty fully accepting that their sins are forgiven when they confess them to God. Why do you think this is true?

Thank God the Father for sending Jesus, the Word incarnate, to us. Ask the Lord who he wants to send you to with the good news. Praise the Father, the Son, and the Holy Spirit for forgiveness of sins and spiritual peace.

NOW OR LATER

Imagine Jesus speaking these same or similar words (John 20:19-23) to you, as he did to these disciples.

- List three or four people the Lord might be sending you to.
- How will he guide you to these people?
- What will you need as you are sent by Jesus to these people—what perspective, motivation, resources, information, and support?

FOUR

STOP DOUBTING AND BELIEVE

John 20:24-31

He confessed, "I was the most reluctant convert in all England." Born in Belfast, Northern Ireland, in 1898, he was poor in math but good in languages as a youngster. He attended church, but at fifteen declared he was "very angry at God for not existing." At Oxford University he earned honors in English literature, ancient history, and classics—becoming a superb literature professor there. He was not a Christian, but Christian colleagues (including J. R. R. Tolkien and G. K. Chesterton) befriended him, listened to him, and discussed with him faith and spiritual topics.

In his book *Surprised by Joy,* he described his journeying to faith after an evening walk:

> Picture me in my room, night after night, feeling, whenever my mind lifted even for a second from my work, the steady, unrelenting approach of Him whom I so earnestly desired not to meet. That which I greatly feared had at last come upon me. In the Trinity Term of 1929 I gave in, admitted God was God, knelt and prayed: perhaps, that night, the most dejected and reluctant convert in all England. . . .
>
> The last stage of my story [is] the transition from mere Theism to Christianity. . . .
>
> When we set out, I did not believe Jesus Christ was the Son of God. When we reached the zoo I did. Yet I had not exactly spent the journey in thought. Nor in great emotion. . . . It was more like a man, after long sleep, still lying motionless in bed, becomes aware that he is now awake. . . . I became a Christian. (C. S. Lewis, *Surprised by Joy,* rev. ed. [New York: Harcourt, Brace, 1995], 221, 224, 229-30)

This is the partial testimony of the famous and widely read twentieth-century Christian writer and apologist, C. S. Lewis. With his clear conversion, his sharp academic mind, and his diverse writing skills, Lewis composed many creative and bestselling works. He became known as, "the apostle to the skeptics"!

After searching and reasoning, C. S. Lewis had come to faith in Jesus Christ. Two thousand years earlier a man questioned the reality of the resurrection, and but after encountering the risen Jesus, he declared his own faith confession and commitment—his name was Thomas.

Group Discussion. Do you think it is okay to ask questions about faith or even have some doubts? Why? Can questions and doubts be a sincere searching or sometimes a resistant façade? Explain.

Personal Reflection. What questions have you had or do you have about Jesus (who he is and what he did)? If you are a Christian, what steps of understanding did you take to your faith commitment?

Thomas, a disciple of Jesus, had a strong leadership personality and was not afraid of or shy about showing his feelings and stating his views. In this study's Scripture, Thomas analyzes and even questions Jesus' statements. *Read John 20:24-31.*

1. Initially, how does Thomas react to the testimonies of the disciples (v. 25)?

2. What are the differences between *doubting* and *disbelief*?

3. A week later, the disciples are again locked in (v. 26), even after the risen Jesus appeared to them on the previous Sunday. What were some possible reasons for this?

4. Compare and contrast believing in Jesus versus being his disciple. How is this spiritual transition and growth observed in the disciples' lives?

5. When people say, "I have a hard time believing in God (or in Jesus)," do you respond, "You just have to believe!" or do you listen to their questions and dialogue with them, sharing with them questions or doubts you had (and conclusions you came to), bringing Scripture, reasoning, examples, and testimonies appropriate to their comments? If you can, give an example.

6. How does Jesus interact with Thomas's questions and doubts (vv. 26-27)?

7. Does Jesus or the Bible promote blind faith? Explain.

8. How does Thomas respond to Jesus?

What can his faith confession mean for you today?

9. What does Jesus tell Thomas that applies to us today?

10. In verses 30-31 John states his purpose for writing this account. Do you find his statement convincing? Explain.

Ask the Lord to increase your understanding and your confidence in the evidence for Jesus' resurrection, and consequently in your personal faith commitment to Jesus Christ as his follower and disciple.

NOW OR LATER

We all at times have some questions or even doubts about our faith. What are things you wish to understand better about Jesus? Share these with the Lord in prayer, and also discuss them with a Christian friend or a pastor.

FIVE

DO YOU LOVE ME?

John 21:1-25

Polycarp was born a few decades after Jesus' death and resurrection, when the young church was growing. A Christian in the Roman province Asia Minor (modern Turkey), he was discipled by the apostle John. In the second century, Polycarp became a bishop whose diocese included Ephesus. A writer and apologist for the expanding faith, his life of integrity and strong faith in Christ—especially expressed at his death—inspired Christians both in his day and through the centuries to our day.

Persecutions of Christians occurred sporadically in Asia Minor. Around AD 155, Bishop Polycarp was brought before the regional Roman proconsul and an angry crowd in the local arena. He would be spared if he acknowledged Caesar as lord publicly and offered incense to Caesar as a demonstration of loyalty. Polycarp refused. Before he was burned at the stake, he reaffirmed his faith in Christ: "Eighty-six years have I served him. . . . How can I blaspheme my King who saved me?" His commitment was not going to be changed, even by his martyrdom (in Greek *martyr* means "witness"). At his death, Polycarp verbally reaffirmed his faith to Jesus as his Savior and his only Lord.

Group Discussion. Do you think a "loyalty oath" to a nation, a group, or a person is proper and productive? Why or why not?

Personal Reflection. Have you ever made or had to make an oath of allegiance? What, when, where, and to whom (or what)? How was the commitment statement worded and administered? Was it difficult to obey? If so, why?

Jesus not only calls individuals to know and follow him but he calls them to fulfill his purposes, which he reiterates with several disciples.

They and we need reminding about what he wants us to be and to do. *Read John 21:1-14.*

1. As in this text, other texts reveal that the resurrected Jesus appeared to many people alone and amid groups in various locations and different times. Why is the diversity of his appearances significant?

2. Using the five *W*s (who, what, where, when, why), give an overview of this story.

3. How does Jesus' interaction with the disciples begin?

4. Why do you think Jesus did not immediately reveal himself?

What evangelism principle or pattern might we learn here from Jesus when starting a religious dialogue with someone?

5. After Peter recognized the person on shore as "the Lord" (v. 7), what happened?

6. Have you come to recognize Jesus as Lord? If so, what changes occurred in your life (thinking, purposes, priorities, behavior, values, or relationships)?

7. What is the significance of Jesus eating breakfast with these disciples?

8. *Read John 21:15-25.* Jesus instructs Peter through a triple question-and-answer exchange. Why do you think Jesus did this (see Luke 22:54-62)?

9. Do you think the Lord's words to Peter (vv. 15-17) apply to all those who love and follow Jesus? If so, in what specific ways?

10. How does Peter react, and how do you think he feels?

11. After Jesus discusses Peter's death, Peter, seeing the beloved disciple, asks, "What about him?" (v. 21). Are there Christians you feel you're in competition with or are compared to? Why?

12. What is the heart and essence of John's account about Jesus the Christ (vv. 24-25), and how does this apply to you and your witness?

Tell the Lord your limitations or weaknesses and even questions about faith. Ask him to guide and enable you to care for, fellowship with, and minister to others.

NOW OR LATER

Where are you in your relationship with Jesus?

- Have you made a faith commitment to him as your Savior and Lord? If so, thank God for the Spirit's work in your mind and heart.
- If not, are you ready to do so now? Or is there an issue or a question you need resolve, and if so, what is it?

The following are some helpful verses about coming to faith in Jesus Christ:

> Yet to all who did receive him, to those who believed in his name, he gave the right to become children of God—children born not of natural descent, nor of human decision or a husband's will, but born of God. (John 1:12-13)

> If you declare with your mouth, "Jesus is Lord," and believe in your heart that God raised him from the dead, you will be saved. (Romans 10:9)

> Therefore, if anyone is in Christ, the new creation has come: The old has gone, the new is here! . . . God was reconciling the world to himself in Christ, not counting people's sins against them. . . . We implore you on Christ's behalf: Be reconciled to God. (2 Corinthians 5:17-20)

> Here I am! I stand at the door and knock. If anyone hears my voice and opens the door, I will come in and eat with that person, and they with me. (Revelation 3:20)

SIX

MAKE DISCIPLES: I AM WITH YOU

Matthew 28:16-20

On **June 20, 1803,** President Thomas Jefferson gave US Army Captain Meriwether Lewis written instruction about the latter's pending westward exploration. In part, the letter says,

> The object of your mission is to explore the Missouri River & such principal streams of it . . . by its course with the water of the Pacific Ocean. Your observations are to be taken with great pains & accuracy, to be entered distinctly & intelligibly for others as well as yourself. . . . In all your intercourse with the natives, treat them in the most friendly & conciliatory manner . . . make them acquainted with the position . . . of the United States of our wish to be neighborly, friendly & useful to them.

Group Discussion. Why do you think Jefferson gave precise instructions for the Lewis and Clark exploration across the North American continent? What were these explorers to do, and how were they to relate to those they encountered?

Personal Reflection. Have you ever been given explicit instructions, written or verbal, for an assignment or project? Summarize its details (what, where, when, how, and why).

At dawn on Easter Sunday "Mary Magdalene and the other Mary" arrived at Jesus' burial site. An angel of the Lord appeared to the women and told them the crucified Jesus had risen. They were to tell the disciples the good news and to meet Jesus in Galilee. Then Jesus appeared in person to the women and repeated the instructions the angel had given them. *Read Matthew 28:16-20.*

1. The interaction of Jesus with his disciples in this Scripture seems to take place toward the end of his forty days of postresurrection appearances. Jesus instructed the disciples to meet him in Galilee. What was special about that region for him and for them?

2. What were the disciples' reactions to the resurrected Jesus (v. 17)?

3. Can a person worship Jesus and yet have some questions? Explain.

4. How might you be like Jesus' disciples in your own faith development and spiritual growth?

5. In Matthew's Gospel account and focus, what are the last words Jesus gives to these disciples?

How does this encouragement and exhortation speak to you today as a Jesus follower?

6. What do Jesus' commissioning words "Go and make disciples of all nations" (v. 19) mean to you?

7. What are some key points from this passage to remember when you share with others the good news about Jesus?

8. What promise does Jesus give these commissioned believers?

Why and how is his promise critical for the disciples and for us as we go out into the world as his servants and witnesses?

9. Who might you start a conversation with about religion, spiritual things, and eventually about Jesus?

Thank God for those who talk with you about Jesus. Ask the Spirit to lead you to family members, friends, neighbors, coworkers, or even strangers you might engage in spiritual discussion and study about Jesus. Also pray how you might grow as a disciple and servant with other Christians.

NOW OR LATER

Who are your friends, family members, coworkers, and neighbors with whom you would like to discuss spiritual topics and ultimately Jesus Christ?

Start praying regularly that the Spirit would

- lead you and these individuals to interact together spiritually.
- give you a listening heart and ear with them.
- open and work in the minds and hearts of these people.
- enable you to have a real dialogue about Jesus.
- lead some them into faith commitments to Jesus.

Note: Rarely will a person come to faith in Jesus during a first talk or conversation. But your initial interaction is the start—just as the disciples first experienced in meeting Jesus and over time became convinced he was the Christ, their Messiah, and their Lord. Friendship and follow-up are important, and prayer is essential as the Spirit works in their lives.

InterVarsity Press booklets are excellent resources for anyone considering Jesus. First read these booklets yourself to strengthen your faith and to know the contents. Then share them with others. When you give them to someone, suggest discussing the booklets in a few days or a week. Then pray for this person's reading and thinking, and also about your pending discussion together.

The following are some booklet suggestions:

- *Christianity for the Open-Minded* (ebook) by Michael Cassidy
- *Have You Considered Him?* by Wilbur Smith
- *What Do We Know About Jesus?* by James Emery White
- *Islam and Christianity* by Donald S. Tingle
- *One Catholic to Another* by Peter Kreeft
- *Are All Religions One?* by Douglas Groothuis
- *The Evidence for the Resurrection* by Norman Anderson
- *Becoming a Christian* by John Stott
- *Why I Believe in Christ* by Charles W. Colson

For more information about these booklets and to order a few, see IVP's website: ivpress.com/ivp-booklets.

SEVEN

WAIT, RECEIVE, WITNESS

Acts 1:1-14

Being a witness can be a challenging—but critical—role and responsibility. If you have participated in an important event, you may be asked to share your experience. If you have observed an accident or a crime, you could be called as a court witness to provide testimony about what you observed.

The following are some guidelines about being a prosecution witness in a Stearns County, Minnesota, courtroom:

- Don't try memorizing what you are going to say. Go over in your mind those matters that will help you recall the incident when you do testify.
- Try to mentally picture the matters about which you will be testifying—such as the place of the incident, objects, people present, what happened, what was said, to whom it was said, at what time, or any other circumstances that may aid you in recalling the events.
- Think before you speak. Make sure you understand each question, and then give an accurate answer. If you don't understand the question, say so or ask to have it repeated.
- If you have to correct your answer, do it right away.
- If you can't recall facts, don't be afraid to say that you cannot recall.

Group Discussion. In trials and court cases, what is the role and importance of witnesses? Are some witnesses more believable than others? Why?

Personal Reflection. Have you ever served on a court jury? What was the case? Describe the witnesses you heard and their creditability. Were you ever called as a witness in a court? What kind of trial, and how was that testifying experience for you?

The book of Acts opens in the springtime, just before the Jewish Feast of Weeks (Acts 2), about forty days after Jesus' crucifixion and resurrection. Before his ascension from earth, Jesus gave his last words and final instructions to his followers—who were still puzzled about what transpired over the past seven weeks and perplexed about what will occur once Jesus is gone. *Read Acts 1:1-14.*

1. Luke, the author of Acts, tells us that his "former book," the Gospel of Luke, was "about all that Jesus began to do and to teach" (v. 1). What is the focus of Luke's second book—Acts?

2. After his death and resurrection but before his ascension, Jesus presented himself to his apostles. Provide some examples of the "many convincing proofs that he was alive" (v. 3) prior to this interaction.

3. While Jesus was eating with the disciples, what command did he give them and why (v. 4)?

4. In response to a question the disciples asked, Jesus summarizes what is unknown about the future (v. 7). How do his words speak to people who predict a day or date for his return or the end of the world?

5. Jerusalem is the starting point for the Jesus community (v. 8). Does the geographic pattern (Jerusalem, Judea, and Samaria, and the ends of the earth) in his instructions apply to us? Explain.

6. After Jesus disappears, two men in white appear beside the disciples (v. 10). What declaration is made about Jesus (v. 11)?

What difference does this statement about Jesus make in your life?

7. We all have questions, doubts, and even assurances about being a witness for Jesus Christ. Name one of yours and discuss it with your group.

8. After Jesus ascended, where did the disciples go (vv. 12-13)?

Who gathered there and why?

9. Are you involved with a Christian group for worship, Bible study, fellowship, prayer, and ministry? If so, how has this group helped you as develop as a Christian?

10. How can you and other Christians pray and reach out to your Jerusalem, Judea and Samaria, and ends of the earth (v. 8)?

Ask the Lord to expand your understanding and application of Jesus' teachings and to extend your witness and service to various areas, groups, and individuals around you.

NOW OR LATER

Study Acts 1:15-26 to learn what the Jerusalem Christians do after Jesus is gone.

To identify how the Lord may be leading and using you, map areas around you (neighborhoods, workplaces, academic environments) and write down names of people you will pray for (family, friends, neighbors, coworkers). Ask the Spirit to open opportunities in these places and with these people to discuss Jesus, and that these persons will be open to believing in and receiving Jesus as their Savior and Lord (John 1:12-13)—and receive fullness life, which is eternal life in him (John 10:10; 17:3; 1 John 1:1-3; 5:11-13).

EIGHT

WHO ARE YOU, LORD?

Acts 9:1-22

Sundar Singh was born in 1889 to a Sikh family. Sikhism is a monotheistic religion but different from Judaism, Christianity, and Islam. From their Punjab village in Northern India, his mother sent him into the jungle miles away to learn from a *sadhu* (an ascetic holy man). Then, so her son would learn English well, she also sent him to a Christian high school.

When Singh was fourteen, his mother died, producing anguish and anger in him. He mocked Christians and became hostile to missionaries. He bought a Bible and then with his friends watching, he burned it. Yet he was searching for existential and spiritual meaning in life. Finally, in desperation he planned to kill himself by jumping in front of an oncoming train.

But the night before his planned suicide, he had a vision and opened his heart to Jesus as his Lord. Consequently, his father rejected him, and his brother tried to poison him. He sought refuge with nearby Christians. He began to wear the national Hindu sadhu attire, a yellow robe and turban, to identify with his homeland Indian culture. Later he studied at an Anglican college, though some Anglican leaders criticized him for not wearing European clerical clothes. He lived a simple, austere life, and sometimes had mystical visions that others were skeptical of. Singh was called "the apostle with bleeding feet" because he continuously walked throughout India communicating the gospel. In 1929 he disappeared into Tibet to share Jesus as Christ—the one he once resisted.

Over two thousand years ago, another man similarly resisted Jesus, opposed the Christian faith, and persecuted Jesus' followers—until he was confronted and changed by the one he was persecuting.

Group Discussion. Do you know individuals whose lives have been transformed by Jesus Christ? Who? What changes have you observed in them? Do you think every Christian must have a sudden conversion experience or a dramatic U-turn in their spiritual experience? Why or why not?

Personal Reflection. What is your relationship or journey with Jesus? If you believe in him, how did this occur, and how are you growing in him? If not yet, ask God to reveal Jesus Christ to you in a fresh and challenging way, as occurred with so many around him and for millennia since.

Saul, or Paul as he would later be called, was an early opponent of Christianity, and he participated in the murder and martyrdom of Stephen, an early Christian leader (see Acts 7:54–8:1). Later, however, the risen Jesus Christ confronts, challenges, and changes the resistant and committed persecutor Saul (Paul). *Read Acts 9:1-22.*

1. Where is Saul (also called Paul in Acts 13:9) going and why (vv. 1-2)?

2. In your own words, recount the interaction between Jesus and Saul on the road to Damascus (vv. 3-6).

3. After his encounter with Jesus, Paul was blind for three days, for "when he opened his eyes he could see nothing" (v. 8). How would you describe Paul's sight before and after this encounter with Jesus?

4. Was there a time in your life when you resisted, ignored, or wondered about Jesus? If you feel comfortable doing so, please share with the group.

5. If you have not had a distinctive, dramatic conversion event, do you feel you have less of a conversion experience or less of a relationship with Jesus? Why or why not?

6. How was the Lord working simultaneously in two places and in two people to confront and to change Paul?

7. What is Ananias's concern, and what words of instruction does the Lord give him?

8. There are several ironies concerning the places and people in this passage? What are some that you can identify?

9. Why is it so important that new Christians—those beginning to follow Jesus—have older, mature believers as friends and mentors?

Have you observed or experienced similar spiritual mentorship? Where, when, and between whom?

10. How do Jesus' words to Paul and to Ananias challenge you as you interact with Christians who are new in their faith or who may have different backgrounds and experiences from you?

11. What does the Lord's leading Paul and Ananias to each other teach you about the Spirit's working and spiritual growth among Christians?

12. Who can you be an "Ananias" to as a friend, encourager, and disciple in Jesus Christ?

Thank God for your encounters and interactions with Jesus Christ—in the past and in these studies—and how specifically these have affected your life. Thank him for people who have assisted you and for those now aiding your growth in faith. Ask the Lord to link you with other Christians, especially those new in their faith, who you might assist as they grow in faith and likeness to Jesus Christ.

NOW OR LATER

Study 1 Samuel 3:1-16. Meditate on Eli's words to young Samuel—to realize the Lord's presence and to respond to his voice: "Speak Lord, your servant is listening" (v. 9). Are you seeking and receptive to Jesus speaking to you?

Study 1 Corinthians 15:1-20. Think through Paul's reasoned presentation about Jesus' resurrection. Are you now more reassured about Jesus' resurrection?

Conclusion: Scan and review these Bible studies. Write down key points and applications.

- In what new and fresh ways have you experienced the risen Jesus Christ?
- How has your Christian faith and life been challenged and confirmed by some of Jesus' last words on earth?

> "Paint Christ not dead, but risen!" cried Tomaso Campanella to the Italian painters of his day [sixteenth and seventeenth centuries]. "Paint Christ, with his foot set in scorn on the rock with which they sought to hold him down! Paint him the conqueror of death! Paint him the Lord of life! Paint him as what he is, the irresistible Victor who, tested to the uttermost, has proved himself in very deed: mighty to save." (Paul Beasley-Murray, *The Message of the Resurrection: Christ Is Risen!* [Downers Grove, IL: InterVarsity Press, 2000], 256)

LEADER'S NOTES

My grace is sufficient for you.

2 CORINTHIANS 12:9

Leading a Bible discussion can be an enjoyable and rewarding experience. But it can also be scary—especially if you've never done it before. If this is your feeling, you're in good company. When God asked Moses to lead the Israelites out of Egypt, he replied, "Please send someone else" (Exodus 4:13)! It was the same with Solomon, Jeremiah, and Timothy, but God helped these people in spite of their weaknesses, and he will help you as well.

You don't need to be an expert on the Bible or a trained teacher to lead a Bible discussion. The idea behind these inductive studies is that the leader guides group members to discover for themselves what the Bible has to say. This method of learning will allow group members to remember much more of what is said than a lecture would.

These studies are designed to be led easily. As a matter of fact, the flow of questions through the passage from observation to interpretation to application is so natural that you may feel that the studies lead themselves. This study guide is also flexible. You can use it with a variety of groups—student, professional, neighborhood, or church groups. Each study takes forty-five to sixty minutes in a group setting.

There are some important facts to know about group dynamics and encouraging discussion. The suggestions listed below should enable you to effectively and enjoyably fulfill your role as leader.

PREPARING FOR THE STUDY

1. Ask God to help you understand and apply the passage in your own life. Unless this happens, you will not be prepared to lead others. Pray too for the various members of the group. Ask God to open your hearts to the message of his Word and motivate you to action.

2. Read the introduction to the guide to get an overview of the entire book and the issues that will be explored.

3. As you begin each study, read and re-read the assigned Bible passage to familiarize yourself with it.

4. This study guide is based on the New International Version of the Bible. It will help you and the group if you use this translation as the basis for your study and discussion.

5. Carefully work through each question in the study. Spend time in meditation and reflection as you consider how to respond.

6. Write your thoughts and responses in the space provided in the study guide. This will help you to express your understanding of the passage clearly.

7. It might help to have a Bible dictionary handy. Use it to look up any unfamiliar words, names, or places. (For additional help on how to study a passage, see chapter five of *How to Lead a LifeGuide Bible Study*, InterVarsity Press.)

8. Consider how you can apply the Scripture to your life. Remember that the group will follow your lead in responding to the studies. They will not go any deeper than you do.

9. Once you have finished your own study of the passage, familiarize yourself with the leader's notes for the study you are leading. These are designed to help you in several ways. First, they tell you the purpose the study guide author had in mind when writing the study. Take time to think through how the study questions work together to accomplish that purpose. Second, the notes provide you with additional background information or suggestions on group dynamics for various questions. This information can be useful when people have difficulty understanding or answering a question. Third, the leader's notes can alert you to potential problems you may encounter during the study.

10. If you wish to remind yourself of anything mentioned in the leader's notes, make a note to yourself below that question in the study.

LEADING THE STUDY

1. Begin the study on time. Open with prayer, asking God to help the group to understand and apply the passage.

2. Be sure that everyone in your group has a study guide. Encourage the group to prepare beforehand for each discussion by reading the introduction to the guide and by working through the questions in the study.

3. At the beginning of your first time together, explain that these studies are meant to be discussions, not lectures. Encourage the members of the group to participate. However, do not put pressure on those who may be hesitant to speak during the first few sessions. You may want to suggest the following guidelines to your group.

- Stick to the topic being discussed.
- Your responses should be based on the verses that are the focus of the discussion and not on outside authorities such as commentaries or speakers.
- These studies focus on a particular passage of Scripture. Only rarely should you refer to other portions of the Bible. This allows for everyone to participate in in-depth study on equal ground.
- Anything said in the group is considered confidential and will not be discussed outside the group unless specific permission is given to do so.
- We will listen attentively to each other and provide time for each person present to talk.
- We will pray for each other.

4. Have a group member read the introduction at the beginning of the discussion.

5. Every session begins with a group discussion question. The question or activity is meant to be used before the passage is read. The question introduces the theme of the study and encourages group members to begin to open up. Encourage as many members as possible to participate, and be ready to get the discussion going with your own response.

This section is designed to reveal where our thoughts or feelings need to be transformed by Scripture. That is why it is especially important not to read the passage before the discussion question is asked. The passage will tend to color the honest reactions people would otherwise give because they are, of course, supposed to think the way the Bible does.

You may want to supplement the group discussion question with an icebreaker to help people get comfortable. See the community section of *Small Group Idea Book* for more ideas.

You also might want to use the personal reflection question with your group. Either allow a time of silence for people to respond individually or discuss it together.

6. Have a group member (or members if the passage is long) read aloud the passage to be studied. Then give people several minutes to read the passage again silently so that they can take it all in.

7. Question 1 will generally be an overview question designed to briefly survey the passage. Encourage the group to look at the whole passage, but try to avoid getting sidetracked by questions or issues that will be addressed later in the study.

8. As you ask the questions, keep in mind that they are designed to be used just as they are written. You may simply read them aloud. Or you may prefer to express them in your own words.

There may be times when it is appropriate to deviate from the study guide. For example, a question may have already been answered. If so, move on to the next question. Or someone may raise an important question not covered in the guide. Take time to discuss it, but try to keep the group from going off on tangents.

9. Avoid answering your own questions. If necessary, repeat or rephrase them until they are clearly understood. Or point out something you read in the leader's notes to clarify the context or meaning. An eager group quickly becomes passive and silent if they think the leader will do most of the talking.

10. Don't be afraid of silence. People may need time to think about the question before formulating their answers.

11. Don't be content with just one answer. Ask, "What do the rest of you think?" or "Anything else?" until several people have given answers to the question.

12. Acknowledge all contributions. Try to be affirming whenever possible. Never reject an answer. If it is clearly off base, ask, "Which verse led you to that conclusion?" or again, "What do the rest of you think?"

13. Don't expect every answer to be addressed to you, even though this will probably happen at first. As group members become more at ease, they will begin to truly interact with each other. This is one sign of healthy discussion.

14. Don't be afraid of controversy. It can be very stimulating. If you don't resolve an issue completely, don't be frustrated. Move on and keep it in mind for later. A subsequent study may solve the problem.

15. Periodically summarize what the group has said about the passage. This helps to draw together the various ideas mentioned and gives continuity to the study. But don't preach.

16. At the end of the Bible discussion you may want to allow group members a time of quiet to work on an idea under "Now or Later." Then discuss what you experienced. Or you may want to encourage group members to work on these ideas between meetings. Give an opportunity during the session for people to talk about what they are learning.

17. Conclude your time together with conversational prayer, adapting the prayer suggestion at the end of the study to your group. Ask for God's help in following through on the commitments you've made.

18. End on time.

Many more suggestions and helps are found in *How to Lead a LifeGuide Bible Study*.

COMPONENTS OF SMALL GROUPS

A healthy small group should do more than study the Bible. There are four components to consider as you structure your time together.

Nurture. Small groups help us to grow in our knowledge and love of God. Bible study is the key to making this happen and is the foundation of your small group.

Community. Small groups are a great place to develop deep friendships with other Christians. Allow time for informal interaction before and after each study. Plan activities and games that will help you get to know each other. Spend time having fun together going on a picnic or cooking dinner together.

Worship and prayer. Your study will be enhanced by spending time praising God together in prayer or song. Pray for each other's needs and keep track of how God is answering prayer in your group. Ask God to help you to apply what you are learning in your study.

Outreach. Reaching out to others can be a practical way of applying what you are learning, and it will keep your group from becoming self-focused. Host a series of evangelistic discussions for your friends or neighbors. Clean up the yard of an elderly friend. Serve at a soup kitchen together, or spend a day working on a Habitat house.

Many more suggestions and helps in each of these areas are found in Small Group Idea Book. Information on building a small group can be found in *Small Group Leaders' Handbook* and *The Big Book on Small Groups* (both from InterVarsity Press). Reading through one of these books would be worth your time.

Before each study, you may want to put an asterisk by the key questions you think are most important for your group to cover, in case you don't have time to cover all the questions. As we suggested in "Getting the Most Out of *The Risen Christ*," if you want to make sure you have enough time to discuss all the questions, you have other options. For example, the group could decide to extend each meeting to ninety minutes or more. Alternatively, you could devote two sixty-minute sessions to each study.

STUDY 1. WHO ARE YOU LOOKING FOR? JOHN 20:1-18

PURPOSE: To observe how the risen Jesus engages someone seeking him, and how he reveals himself to the sad and surprised Mary Magdalene, whose faith and actions are dramatically changed.

Background information. Joseph of Arimathea was a member of the Jewish Sanhedrin, the council that provided leadership for Jews even under their occupation by the Romans. He had become a follower of Jesus (Matthew 27:57-61; John 19:38-42). All four Gospels record that he requested Jesus' body from Pilate, the Roman governor, and buried it in his own tomb after he and Nicodemus anointed it with spices and wrapped it in linen cloth.

After following Joseph and seeing precisely where Jesus was placed (Mark 15:47; Luke 23:55), the women followers of Jesus went home. It was almost sunset Friday when the Jewish Sabbath rest and worship began. These women would prepare spices and perfumes to anoint Jesus' body, countering its decaying odors and contributing to the body's decomposition.

Questions 2-3. This Mary is from the village of Magdala. She is mentioned as one of the women who supported Jesus and his disciples "out of their own means" (Luke 8:3), and Jesus had cast seven demons out of her (Luke 8:2). All four Gospels tell of Mary's presence at Jesus' tomb and proclamation of his resurrection. "Later tradition identified Mary Magdalene with the sinful women who anointed Jesus in the house of the Pharisee (Lk 7:36-50), but this identification cannot be proved" (Paul Beasley-Murray, *The Message of the Resurrection* [Downers Grove, IL: InterVarsity Press, 2000], 84).

The "first day of the week, while it was still dark" (v. 1) is predawn Sunday. For the Jews, the seventh day of the week was Saturday, the Jewish Sabbath (when God rested after creation [see Genesis 2:2-3]). The morning sun was about to rise, but the mourned Son is already up!

Most scholars agree "the other disciple" (vv. 2-3, 8) is John the apostle and this Gospel's writer (see John 13:23; 19:26; 21:20).

Question 4. This is a sad and shocking time for Mary and all of Jesus' followers. Mary is not only in a period of mourning but she is in a state of shock (vv. 11-15). At the tomb they are despondent and distraught because Jesus' body is gone.

> Jewish people took the first seven days of mourning so seriously that mourners could not wash, work, have intercourse or even study the law. Jewish culture was serious about expressing rather than repressing grief. That the body is missing and thus people are prevented from bestowing final acts of love would be regarded as intolerably tragic; even tomb robbers usually left the body behind. (Craig S. Keener, *The IVP Bible Background Commentary: New Testament* [Downers Grove, IL: InterVarsity Press, 1993], 316).

Question 6. Mary assumed the second questioner, Jesus, was a gardener, a common laborer who would have been there to tend the tomb area, not to watch or guard the tomb and the body.

Reacting to a loved one's death, some people express their grief with tears (Mary), but others may not (Peter and John). Neither response necessarily reflects greater or lesser feelings for a deceased loved one. Mary went to minister to a dead body, but a live body—the resurrected Jesus Christ—ministers to her.

Question 7. "Who [or what] is it you are looking for?" (v. 15) is the key for any spiritual quest. Jesus asked this of John the Baptist's disciples (John 1:38-39), inviting them to come and see who he is. At the turning point in his life and ministry, Jesus asked his own disciples, "Who do people say I am?" and then "Who do you say I am?" (Mark 8:27, 29; Luke 9:18, 20). Faith in Jesus must be personal commitment and involvement, not secondhand communication or information.

Question 8. The New International Version's "Do not hold on to me" (v. 17) is a better translation than the King James Version that reads: "Touch me not." Encountering Jesus alive, Mary wants to hug him and not let him go. But he must show himself alive and speak to other people. Also Mary must go from the empty tomb to explain to other followers, "I have seen the Lord!" (v. 18). This is the Easter proclamation.

> It is most likely that the verb translated *hold* (17) is to be understood in the sense "do not continue to grasp hold of me." This would not be in contradiction with the initiation to Thomas in v. 27. . . . The fact is that "touching" is not the basis of ongoing faith. . . . Jesus told Mary to announce "I am ascending" (rather than *returning*) in the sense of a continuing process which had not yet reached its climax. . . . When Mary announced her experience (18) she was more concerned with her meeting with the Lord than with the message about the ascension. (D. A. Carson, R. T. France, J. A. Motyer, and G. J. Wenham, eds., *New Bible Commentary 21st Century Edition* [Downers Grove, IL: InterVarsity Press, 1994], 1063)

Question 10. Be sensitive to those who are willing to tell the group about their encounters with Jesus and even questions about him. Don't criticize their personal experience. As a follow-up question, you might ask if the members of the group are open to such an encounter with Jesus now or in the future. Perhaps he will reveal himself during these studies.

Question 11. When Mary goes to the disciples, she tells what she knows. She does not have every spiritual or theological answer, but she shares her personal experience with the risen Christ. Women's testimony in the ancient world held little value, yet Jesus first appeared to and relied on the testimony of Mary Magdalene!

> A strong historical case for the resurrection can provide a powerful antidote to the persuasive view today, held by many believers and unbelievers, that religion in general and Christianity in particular isn't about evidence but about (blind) faith. Nothing could be further from the truth—or more effective at rendering Christian thought intellectually irrelevant. (David Baggett, ed., *Did the Resurrection Happen? A Conversation with Gary Habermas and Antony Flew* [Downers Grove, IL: InterVarsity Press, 2009], 20)

STUDY 2. WHAT ARE YOU DISCUSSING? LUKE 24:13-49

PURPOSE: To observe how Jesus engages people and learns what they know about him, and then to understand what he says about himself now that he is alive after being dead.

Background information. Israelites celebrated three great festivals annually per God's instructions through Moses (Exodus 23:14-17; 34:18-23; Deuteronomy 16:1-17):

1. Passover: To recall and to praise God for the angel of death passing over the Israelite slave homes in Egypt (Exodus 12), and for their exodus liberation out of Egypt. It is celebrated in springtime.

2. Pentecost or Weeks: To celebrate spring harvest of wheat and barley, fifty days after Passover and before the Festival of Booths.

3. Booths or Tabernacles: To mark the start of spring harvest. Farmers often built and lived in temporary shelters recalling their ancestors' forty-year wilderness encampment. Some Jews still do this today.

Question 1. Could these "two" walkers, heading home after the Passover weekend, possibly be a husband and wife (the text does not say "two men")? Couples and families traveled to Jerusalem for key religious events. Jesus' parents took him as a baby and twelve years later as a young boy to the Jewish capital city (Lk 2:22-52). A few scholars suggest Jesus was not recognized (v. 16) by these two because they were walking westward toward a bright setting sun. Others speculate their grief caused blurred vision. But when they arrived home, they still didn't know it was Jesus. Perhaps their problem was spiritual blindness.

Question 2. As in this case, when Jesus engages people, he often starts with questions, not answers. For example: Mary at the tomb

(John 20:14-17), the woman at the well (John 4:5-7), and his apostles at Caesarea Philippi (Luke 9:18-25). Before he discusses faith and himself, he needs to know what others think. Evangelism is often more listening than talking! Christians should not do dump-truck evangelism—backing into individuals, unloading the gospel, and then pulling away. We should listen and learn what others think before sharing the good news, applicable Scriptures, theological points, and our own testimony.

Question 7. "Jesus continued on as if he were going farther" (v. 28). Was Jesus being polite, or was he testing their spiritual interest? It was almost dark, and bandits could threaten travelers, especially at night. A foundational Middle Eastern virtue is to always offer home hospitality, food, and accommodations.

Question 10. Jesus and the religious authorities may have disagreed about biblical interpretations, but he and they agreed on the Scripture's authority. Here, with his troubled disciples, he "opened their minds so they could understand the Scriptures" (v. 45), as he had with the Emmaus couple (v. 27), about his being the promised Messiah through the three sections of Jewish Scripture: the Law of Moses, the Prophets, and the Writings.

When we explain Scripture (v. 27) it should bring understanding of the Scriptures about Christ, repentance, and forgiveness (vv. 45-47). We should not attempt to win theological arguments or demonstrate our great Bible knowledge. Rather we should dialogue with and pray for others that they may meet Jesus in Scripture and then invite him as Lord in their lives by faith.

Those encountering the risen Jesus, then as now, have burning hearts (v. 32) and opened minds (v. 45). The direction of their lives is reversed.

Questions 11-12. Both to the couple going to Emmaus and to his disciples huddled in Jerusalem, Jesus shows himself risen in the flesh and revealed in Scripture. Jesus wants them—and us—to understand his resurrection from the dead and also his good news message, which he passes to all believers. As he explained and we should help others see, all the Scriptures testify to Jesus as the Messiah (the Christ) of God—to which we are to be witnesses.

STUDY 3. I AM SENDING YOU. JOHN 20:19-23

PURPOSE: To learn what peace the risen Jesus Christ grants his disciples and what purpose he gives them.

Background information. John 20:1-18 reveals that the Passover weekend was traumatic for the disciples. Jesus was arrested, tried, convicted, beaten, and crucified. Their leader and Lord was dead. But then word spread among a few disciples on this Easter Sunday that Jesus is risen and alive, and that he had encountered a few followers around dawn and again in the late afternoon! Now it is evening and the gathered disciples are still sad, stunned, and stupefied.

Question 1. The disciples were behind "doors locked for fear" (v. 19). If authorities arrested Jesus with false charges and crucified him, then might they not seek the same fate for his followers?

Question 4. The disciples were fearful of the authorities who had just killed their leader, Jesus. So they are "locked-in" and almost trapped by their fears. We all can get into situations when we feel surrounded and pressed in by other people, by circumstances, by our own mistakes, or by pressures real or imagined. Jesus' unexpected appearance among them cause them to be overwhelmed *and* "overjoyed" (v. 20).

Question 6. God the Father sent Jesus the Son into the world "full of grace and truth" (John 1:14) to declare and to demonstrate that the kingdom of God has come (Matthew 3:2). Now, similarly, Jesus is sending his disciples into the world to share and to show his good news. "As the Father has sent me, I am sending you" (John 20:21). As we are sent, we should all reflect Jesus' characteristics as his couriers.

Question 8. Then "he breathed on them and said, 'Receive the Holy Spirit'" (v. 22). This differs from the Spirit coming upon thousands at Pentecost in Acts 2. In that latter event, the Spirit comes upon many believers as the good news is preached and heard amid a huge gathering, whereas here Jesus focuses on these apostolic leaders of his church and first proclaimers of his gospel. Note the Greek word for *spirit* can also mean "wind" or "breath." This passage brings thoughts of God the Creator breathing life into the first human beings (Genesis 2:7) and the Spirit breathing life into the dry bones in a valley (Ezekiel 37:1-10).

> Jesus breathes on the disciples, as the Creator breathed into human nostrils at the beginning [creation]. They are equipped to be people through whom forgiveness of sins becomes a reality in the world. They are thereby sent into the world, as the father had sent Jesus, . . . by their witness to him—the unique and decisive events of his ministry, his death, [and] his resurrection. (N. T. Wright, *The Resurrection of the Son of God*, Christian Origins and the Question of God 3 [Minneapolis, MN: Fortress Press, 2003], 671)

Question 10. Scripture never teaches that human beings forgive sin, though we proclaim the forgiveness of sins as we proclaim the gospel. Only God (Psalm 103:12; Isaiah 43:25; Daniel 9:9; Micah 7:18-19) and Jesus (1 John 1:9; Colossians 1:13-14) can forgive sins—as people respond to the good news. Note in Mark 2:5-7, 10, that some religious teachers become angry when Jesus tells the paralytic "your sins are forgiven" (v. 5) because they think Jesus is blaspheming—"Who can forgive sins but God alone!" (v. 7). Our theological and ecclesiastical understanding is that clergy do not forgive sins—they only attest to this and affirm it in Jesus Christ.

STUDY 4. STOP DOUBTING AND BELIEVE. JOHN 20:24-31

PURPOSE: To observe Jesus' response to questions and doubts from people (like Thomas), and to understand the reason for John's written account about Jesus.

Background information. Thomas is not a shy, quiet disciple, but has a strong personality and is willing to speak up (see, for example, John 11:1-16; 14:1-6). Jesus chose strong personalities as his apostles and leaders in training. So *doubter* may not be the most accurate adjective for Thomas. Rather *questioner* might be a better term, for he seeks reasonable and solid evidence for his faith if he is going to follow Jesus.

Questions 1-3. The disciples, even after encountering Jesus alive, are still fearful. Why was Thomas not present the first Sunday afternoon when Jesus appeared among these disciples? Maybe Thomas had given up, maybe he was afraid, or maybe he just needed to be alone to analyze what has happened. But by cutting himself out of Christian fellowship and community, he missed out on Jesus' appearance and his interaction with the others. Again they are behind locked doors (vv. 19, 26). The risen Jesus Christ passes though locked doors, stands among them, and speaks to them. Again, he greets them with his "peace" (v. 26). A week has passed and they "stay in the city" as Jesus instructed them (Luke 24:49; see study 5 and Acts 1:4), waiting for the promised outpouring of the Holy Spirit.

Question 6. Jesus, as he frequently did, initiates the interaction to welcome seekers and questioners. He knows Thomas's thoughts and doubts. He invites Thomas to touch where he was nailed and speared (v. 27). Crucifixion death was caused by a day or two of respiratory stress and exposure exhaustion. A crucified person who hung on a cross would slightly raise their body for more air. If the nails were driven through the small hand bones, when the person slumped back downward his body weight would probably cause his hands to tear open. Therefore nails were more likely driven through the wrists (the term or reference to "hands" can also include wrists). Since the Jews asked Pilate to take down all the crucified bodies because the next day was a special Passover Sabbath (John 19:31-37), a soldier speared the side of Jesus to ensure he was dead before removing him from his cross.

Jesus encourages this disciple, and any inquirer, to "reach out," investigate, and then to "stop doubting and believe" (v. 27). Do we welcome such seekers and doubters, or do we distrust and stifle them?

Thomas's statement of faith is one of the great confessions and commitments in the Bible, "My Lord and my God!" (v. 28). Jesus meets Thomas's uncertainty with certitude by personal encounter with his followers. Thomas's doubts about the resurrection are dissolved, and his belief in Jesus is buttressed.

> In the Fourth Gospel Thomas is a hardheaded realist who exemplifies the disciples' lack of understanding (11:16) and their confusion (14:5). . . . [His] response is astonishing . . . [and] his confession "[You are] my Lord and my God" goes beyond affirming the reality of the resurrection to interpreting its significance [for him personally]. (G. R. Osborne, "Resurrection," in *Dictionary of Jesus and the Gospels*, ed. Joel B. Green, Scot McKnight, and I. Howard Marshall [Downers Grove, IL: IVP Academic, 1992], 686).

Question 9. Doubt is usually more wondering, pondering, deliberating, questioning, or probing. In contrast, disbelief is more suspicion, skepticism, distrust, denial, resistance, and rejection. The former suggests openness to evidence and reason; the latter reveals a person who is closed to such data and possibilities.

Question 10. Most nonfiction authors state their reason for writing at their work's beginning. John states his purpose for compiling and writing this Gospel account: "[1] that you may believe that Jesus is the Messiah, the Son of God, and [2] that by believing you may have life in his name." The Gospel of John tells readers that by believing and receiving Jesus Christ, one has a new life "born of God" (John 1:12-13) to "enter the kingdom of God" (John 3:3-8) and that this life is "full" or "more abundant" (John 10:10) and "eternal" (John 17:1-3).

Over the centuries some critics suggest that Jesus did not rise from the dead. But Christian faith rests (or dies) on the question and reality of Jesus being raised from the dead. For a concise analysis of questions about the resurrection, get Norman Anderson's excellent booklet *The Evidence for the Resurrection* (Downers Grove, IL: InterVarsity Press, 1966). It is important to analyze these faith challenges and speculative theories, answering with facts and reason to counter them.

Asking questions with an open mind to learn about Jesus is productive: "Ask and it will be given to you; seek and you will find; knock and the door will be opened to you" (Jesus' words in Matthew 7:7). Such seekers will not only find answers but will encounter the risen and living Jesus. (See the suggested IVP booklets at the end of study 6 to give to seekers and to strengthen Christians).

STUDY 5. DO YOU LOVE ME? JOHN 21:1-25

PURPOSE: To learn how Jesus encounters and encourages his disciples in everyday settings, and what instructions and explanations he gives them for their lives and future ministries.

Background information. Peter was probably the key leader among the twelve disciples Jesus called to be his colleagues, trainees, ministry team, and future leaders of the church. But even with his strong personality and definitive statements, he failed Jesus—he denied that he knew Jesus. No doubt he feared for his life, as did other followers of Jesus, for his leader and Lord was arrested and being interrogated by Jewish and Roman authorities. According to the Scripture, Peter was not near Jesus' crucifixion; neither were any male disciples except John (John 19:25-27). Yet Jesus appeared risen to his followers and later he renewed fellowship with Peter (John 21).

Question 1. Visions of a deceased famous or religious person usually occur to just one or only a few individuals, such as devotees hoping for sightings. But Jesus appears, at different times and in various locations, to many individuals and groups who were not expecting to see him again.

Question 3-4. "Friends, haven't you any fish?" (v. 5) is a conversation starter—Jesus again initiates interaction. This is a subtle entrée for more discussion about the missions on which Jesus will soon send these disciples. When he originally called them, Jesus said his new followers would "fish for people" (Matthew 4:19). Elsewhere, he even directed them where to fish, "put out into deep water" (Luke 5:4-7), as he does here.

We should pray about where we are "fishing" or casting our nets for religious dialogues and discussions. For suggestions to start spiritual conversations, see Paul Little's excellent books *How to Give Away Your Faith* and *Know Why You Believe* (both by InterVarsity Press).

Question 5. After John tells Peter, "It is the Lord" (v. 7), Peter wraps his "outer garment" (removed for fishing) over his loincloth. (Jews were never naked in public, as Greek wrestlers or Romans could be in spas.) Then he "jumped into the water" (v. 7) and swam or waded through this shallow water "about a hundred yards" to the lakeside beach (v. 8).

Question 8. What comparison is Jesus making when he questions Peter, "Do you love me more than these?" No doubt this reminds Peter of his statement to Jesus and among the other disciples at the Last Supper: "Even if all [others] fall away on account of you, I never will. . . . I will never disown you" (Matthew 26:33, 35). But he did! When we become prideful, we fall (Proverbs 16:18; 1 Corinthians 10:12). Yet Jesus' present threefold directive replaces Peter's past threefold denial.

Some writers emphasize the two different Greek words used here for "love"—*phileō* and *agapaō*—(vv. 15-17) asked three times by Jesus. But many scholars say these two words are interchangeable, and Jesus is not creating word nuances but rather his exhortation is: if you are committed to me, then you will care for my sheep.

Question 11. When we become quite elderly, someone may need to dress and guide us. Was this a play on words or an allusion by Jesus to Peter's death (v. 18, "stretch out your hands . . . dress you and lead you where you do not want to go")? Church traditions say that Peter was bound and crucified upside down in Rome around AD 62, but in contrast John died an old man and Christian leader in Ephesus, probably in the 90s. Many early followers of Jesus were killed for their faith.

Peter raises the comparison himself. Most scholars concur that the "him" (v. 21) is John the apostle and the Gospel writer. There is a human tendency to compare ourselves with others. We all do this, like Peter (vv. 20-23), maybe it is from envy or from ego, maybe it is from inferiority feelings or because of superiority attitudes. But Jesus calls us to follow him, not others—to compare ourselves to him, not to other people.

Question 12. Verifying testimonies was very important in the ancient world in court cases, in public forums, and in documents. So John, in his concluding statement (v. 24), affirms this written account is true and reliable.

STUDY 6. MAKE DISCIPLES. MATTHEW 28:16-20

PURPOSE: To comprehend the risen Lord Jesus' authority and assignment to his apostles—and to us—and to have confidence in his appearance and words.

Background information. Making disciples or followers is a common practice of many leaders, ancient or modern. But the method and purpose of Jesus was different than that of Jewish leaders:

> "Making disciples" was the sort of thing rabbis would do, but Jesus' followers are to make disciples for Jesus, not for themselves. . . .
>
> Many Jews outside Palestine sought converts among the "nations" (which can also be translated "Gentiles" or "pagans"). But only a few converts ever studied under rabbis, so the idea of making Gentiles full disciples—followers of Jesus who would learn from and serve him—goes beyond the Jewish tradition. (Craig S. Keener, "Matthew 28:19-20," *Bible Background Commentary: New Testament* [Downers Grove, IL: InterVarsity Press, 2004], 130-31)

Question 1. At the start of his ministry when Jesus prayed and called twelve men as his apostles (Mark 3:13-19)—to be with him and to be sent out (v. 14)—he did so on a Galilean mountainside. We don't know which mountainside that was, but it could have been the one mentioned in our passage, on which he now commissions them for their future mission and ministries as his ambassadors.

Question 2. The Gospels do not portray the apostles and early believers as unflawed in their faith. Rather these women and men are described as normal, imperfect human beings. It took much time and many interactions with Jesus, before and after his resurrection, and the Holy Spirit's empowerment for his followers to solidify their faith in him as their Lord and to start ministries for him as their leader.

The same Greek word here for "doubted" (v. 17) is also used in Matthew 14:31, when Peter wavered as he tried to walk on water to Jesus (Matthew 14:22-33). Thus this word may denote less an intellectual unbelief and more of a natural hesitation when encountering a challenging situation. *The Message* version says: "The moment they saw him they worshiped him. Some, though, held back, not sure . . . about risking themselves totally" (v. 17). They are still growing in their faith and confidence, and Jesus encourages them, "I am with you always" (v. 20). After Jesus' ascension and the Spirit's descent on believers, his disciples go out into the world and make disciples—risking their own lives.

Question 5-6. The two components of the Great Commission are (1) taking new believers into the church, and (2) instructing them in the Christian faith. So Jesus commands these leaders to baptize and teach new believers "of all nations" (v. 19). Even if we are not clergy, we all should be participating in this disciple-making, two-stage process, as Christ directed.

STUDY 7. WAIT, RECEIVE, WITNESS. ACTS 1:1-14

PURPOSE: To understand Jesus' words to his followers about waiting for his timing, and to grasp his purposes in the Holy Spirit's power for involvement in his workings.

Background information. In the Old Testament, the Spirit of God would be poured out on individuals in certain leadership roles or for specific tasks. But the hope was that one day the Holy Spirit would be poured out on all of his people. The prophet Joel prophesied it (Joel 2:28-29), Jesus promised it (John 14:16-17, 25-27; 15:26-27; 16:5-15; Acts 1:4-5), and Pentecost provided it for believers (Acts 2:1-21). The Spirit's coming personally meant the kingdom coming powerfully. John Stott summarizes well what the kingdom issues were in Jesus' last words with these leaders:

> The kingdom of God is not a territorial concept. It does not—and cannot—figure on any map. Yet this is what the apostles were still envisaging by confusing the kingdom of God with the kingdom of Israel. . . .
>
> What Jesus rebukes them for was not their expectation of a national kingdom but only their desire to know "times and dates," together perhaps with their consequent lack of concern for world mission. (John Stott, *The Spirit, the Church, and the World: The Message of Acts* [Downers Grove, IL: InterVarsity Press, 1990], 41)

Question 1. If your group is having difficulty answering this question, point them to verse 8.

Question 2. You can help the group with this question by reminding them of Jesus' appearances to the two disciples on their way to Emmaus (see study 2), to the disciples and Thomas in the locked room (see study 4), and to the disciples in Galilee when they had no luck fishing (see study 5). You can also ask them to read 1 Corinthians 15:3-7, where Paul discusses Jesus' appearances.

Question 4. Specific predictions about Jesus' return or his second coming have always proved false—and are proposed unwisely—because Jesus said, "It is not for you [us] to know the times or dates" (v. 7).

Unlike Jews' hope for national freedom and political independence from Roman occupiers, Jesus taught and brought the kingdom of God, which is spiritual, communal, and personal (and, of course, has political implications). The kingdom of God and its spread are not through force but through faith, not because of wars but because of witnesses, not in power but in proclamation, not via great weapons but through good works, not by human strength but by the Lord's Spirit.

Question 10. In his powerful chapter about the resurrection (1 Corinthians 15), Paul reviews the essential elements "of first [primary] importance" in Jesus' life: "that Christ died for our sins, . . . that he was buried, . . . that he was raised on the third day, . . . and that he appeared to Cephas [Peter], and then to the Twelve. After that, he appeared to more than five hundred of the brothers and sisters, . . . most of whom are still living" (vv. 3-6). Thus, the risen Jesus appeared to many people who could be questioned about his being alive. His appearances and words were vital to validate his resurrection.

STUDY 8. WHO ARE YOU, LORD? ACTS 9:1-22

PURPOSE: To learn how the risen Jesus confronts his persecutor and changes him into his proclaimer, and to see how the Lord works simultaneously through different people in different places for his purposes.

Background. Paul's conversion is the most famous in Christian history. In Acts, Luke tells this story three times: once in his own summary (Acts 9:1-19) and twice reporting Paul's two verbal testimonies (Acts 22:1-16; 26:1-23). Paul also gives another account of his conversion in Galatians 1:11-24.

Question 1. Paul, who had been known as Saul (see Acts 13:9), was a well-educated Pharisee (Acts 22:1-5; Gal 1:13-14). He was determined to defend Judaism and to destroy any deviation from it. He obtained official documents to introduce himself to other Jewish leaders and to round up, with synagogue leaders' assistance, those he believed to be heretics—that is, these followers of Jesus as their Messiah.

> A letter with similar purpose has been preserved in the Apocrypha: *"If any scoundrels have fled to you, hand them to the high priest Simon, so that he may punish them according to their law"* (1 Maccabees 15:21 [in the second century before Christ]). Many Jewish congregations would not have felt quite as negatively about the Christians, and these letters from the high priest may have outlined the Jewish objections to Christianity as well as giving Paul authority to make *prisoners* of these "criminals." (See 28:21-22, where the Jewish leaders in Rome [meeting with Paul] knew they were supposed to dislike the Christians but had no "letters from Judea" telling them why.) (G. J. Wenham, J. A. Motyer, D. A. Carson, and R. T. France, eds., *New Bible Commentary*, 21st-Century Edition [Downers Grove, IL: InterVarsity Press, 1994], 1080)

Approximately ten thousand Jews lived in Damascus at this time. Jesus' followers were also there: those "who belonged to the Way" (v. 2), which was a designation for early Christians (see Acts 22:4; 24:14, 22), which may have come from Jesus' pre-crucifixion words, "I am the way and the truth and the life" (John 14:6). Apparently the name "Christians" first occurred at Antioch (Acts 11:26).

Question 2. Jesus' challenge to Saul, who hears a voice addressing him (Acts 9:4-5),

> was more than a question—It was an accusation. The way the question is framed is condemning. Jesus didn't ask why Saul was persecuting the church; he asked why Saul was persecuting *him*. . . . Had Jesus [previously] tried a gentler form of persuasion that Saul ignored? We're not told. . . . Now direct confrontation was needed. (Alton Gansky, *30 Events That Shaped the Church: Learning from Scandal, Intrigue, and Revival* [Grand Rapids: Baker, 2015], 25-26)

A few speculate about what was behind Paul's conversion. Luke's report (Luke 9:1-9) and Paul's own accounts (Acts 22:6-11; 26:12-18) affirm the bodily appearance of the resurrected Jesus Christ.

> [Luke's and Paul's] accounts dovetail quite well. But the historical conclusion . . . cannot be that Paul did not see Jesus (which neither of them say) or that he "saw" Jesus only with his mind or heart (which, again, neither of them say), or that he saw Jesus simply as a "being of light" (which, once more, neither of them say). . . . Paul says that he saw Jesus, and that remains our primary historical datum. (N. T. Wright, *The Resurrection of the Son of God*, Christian Origins and the Question of God 3 [Minneapolis, MN: Fortress Press, 2003], 393)

Question 3. Blindness can be both physical and spiritual. Surely Paul's blindness is both, as he is coming to faith in Jesus the Christ. It might be helpful to review the story of the healing of the blind man in John 9, which is also about "spiritual blindness" in people.

Questions 6-7. Ananias is quite apprehensive about Paul because of reports about "all the harm he has done to [God's] holy people [Jesus believers] in Jerusalem" (v. 13). When some women and men accept

Jesus Christ, their past behaviors and attitudes (especially anti-Christian ones) can cause others to doubt and question their new profession of faith (like Paul here).

> When Chuck Colson became a Christian, the whole nation reacted with skepticism—Christians and non-Christians alike. Of the leading characters in the Watergate scandal, he was one of the most notorious. Could such a calculating man sincerely come to God? (*NIV Quiet Time Bible: New Testament* [Downers Grove, IL: InterVarsity Press, 1994], 182)

Yet the Lord works through the Holy Spirit to change individuals through many ways and through various people, even those unknown to each other, drawing them together in Jesus Christ for his spiritual purposes.

Question 8. There are many ironies here. Paul will be discipled in the home of a man whose name (v. 11) is like the name of the Lord's betrayer, Judas (Luke 22:3-6; Mark 14:43-46). The home where Paul will begin his growth as a new believer in Jesus is located on Straight Street (v. 11), which is a figurative description of his new direction and spiritual life in Christ. The disciple instrumental in the beginning of Paul's Christian life and growth (vv. 17-19) is Ananias, which is the same name (1) of a man, Ananias, who lied to the apostles, "to the Holy Spirit," and "to God" (Acts 5:3-4) about the money he was donating from a land sale, and also later (2) the high priest Ananias, who interrogated the prisoner Paul before the Sanhedrin (Acts 23:1-10). Finally, the Damascus synagogues where Paul sought leaders to help him persecute Christians (v. 2) were the synagogues where he began proclaiming Jesus as the Messiah to listeners (Acts 9:20-22).

Questions 10-11. Roads and routes to conversion differ, but the reality of commitment to Jesus Christ is the same because of his resurrection, forgiveness of sin, and newness of life in the Holy Spirit. A Jewish man who became a Christian in college after an intense intellectual and spiritual search—reading scholars, skeptics, and Scripture—summarizes the crux of Jesus' resurrection:

> Yet, if the resurrection remains in the academic realm of debate, theological or historical, it remains dead. The issue of Jesus' resurrection is deeply personal and communal. It is about God's love for

> us, and God's plan for our lives, as individuals and as a people. . . . It should evoke in us conversion. We should not . . . simply try to ignore it. Rather, we must reflect on how these truths impact our way of life and being. (Jeffrey Morrow, *Jesus' Resurrection: A Jewish Convert Examines the Evidence*, Principium Institute Historical Background to the Bible [Toledo, OH: Principium Institute, 2017], 75-76)

Personally meeting and committing to the risen Christ as our Savior and Lord—however it occurs, gradually or suddenly—is the essence of knowing, following, and serving him in our lives. John Stott assesses this well:

> "I have had no Damascus Road experience," many people say. . . . [But] in order to be converted, it is not necessary for us to be struck by divine lightning, or fall to the ground, or hear our name called out in Aramaic, any more than it is necessary to travel to precisely the same place [as Paul's conversion] outside Damascus. Nor is it possible to be granted a resurrection appearance or call to apostleship like Paul's. It is clear from the rest of the New Testament that other features of Saul's conversion and commissioning are applicable to us. We too can and must experience a personal encounter with Jesus Christ, surrender to him in repentance and faith, and receive his summons to service. (John Stott, *The Spirit, the Church, and the World: The Message of Acts* [Downers Grove, IL: InterVarsity Press, 1990], 165-66)

Bill Weimer, formerly a Navy chaplain, is pastor emeritus of Mariner Sands Chapel, an ecumenical congregation in Stuart, Florida. In the 1960s he became an active Christian through InterVarsity Christian Fellowship, and his wife, Eathel (Bowie), was one of the first female InterVarsity staff workers in the South. For more than five decades they have led Bible discussions on college campuses, at military commands, and for six congregations. They now live in Atlantic Beach, Florida, where they participate in various Scripture studies.